YOU KNOW YOU'RE A COMPUTER NERD WHEN . . .

Net Addict

SUMMERSDALE

Summersdale Publishers Ltd
46 West Street
Chichester
West Sussex
PO19 1RP
United Kingdom

www.summersdale.com

ISBN 1 84024 136 5

Printed and bound in Great Britain

Cartoons by Kate Taylor

YOU KNOW YOU'RE A COMPUTER NERD WHEN . . .

Every sentence you utter begins with, 'On the Net. . .'

YOU KNOW YOU'RE A COMPUTER NERD WHEN . . .

Your partner makes a new rule: 'The computer cannot come to bed.'

YOU KNOW YOU'RE A COMPUTER NERD WHEN . . .

You are doing more and more things that you swore you would never do when you first got on-line.

YOU KNOW YOU'RE A COMPUTER NERD WHEN . . .

Tech Support calls *you* for help.

YOU KNOW YOU'RE A COMPUTER NERD WHEN . . .

Your other half says, 'Communication is important in a marriage,' so you buy another computer and install a second phone line so the two of you can chat.

YOU KNOW YOU'RE A COMPUTER NERD WHEN . . .

You wake up at 4 a.m. to go to the toilet and stop to check your e-mail on the way back to bed.

YOU KNOW YOU'RE A COMPUTER NERD WHEN . . .

You have a tattoo that reads, 'This person best viewed with Internet Explorer 5.0 or higher.'

YOU KNOW YOU'RE A COMPUTER NERD WHEN . . .

You turn off your modem and get an awful empty feeling.

YOU KNOW YOU'RE A COMPUTER NERD WHEN . . .

You marry your cyber-girlfriend/boyfriend and then both sit at your own computers and chat to each other from across the room.

YOU KNOW YOU'RE A COMPUTER NERD WHEN . . .

YOU KNOW YOU'RE A COMPUTER NERD WHEN . . .

You set your kitchen on fire while cooking dinner because you wanted to 'check your mail' and while there, you 'just wanted to see who was on-line'.

YOU KNOW YOU'RE A COMPUTER NERD WHEN . . .

You find yourself typing 'com' after every full stop when using a word processor.

YOU KNOW YOU'RE A
COMPUTER NERD WHEN . . .

You refer to going to the
toilet as downloading.

YOU KNOW YOU'RE A COMPUTER NERD WHEN . . .

YOU KNOW YOU'RE A COMPUTER NERD WHEN . . .

All of your close friends have an @ in their names.

YOU KNOW YOU'RE A COMPUTER NERD WHEN . . .

At work, your boss constantly reminds you that the word 'i' should be capitalised.

YOU KNOW YOU'RE A COMPUTER NERD WHEN . . .

You wake up in the morning and the first thing you do, even before you have your first cup of coffee, is get on-line.

YOU KNOW YOU'RE A COMPUTER NERD WHEN . . .

You can't contact your mother . . . she doesn't have a modem.

YOU KNOW YOU'RE A COMPUTER NERD WHEN . . .

You no longer type with proper capitalisation, punctuation, or complete sentences.

YOU KNOW YOU'RE A COMPUTER NERD WHEN . . .

You want to be buried with your computer when you die or vice versa.

YOU KNOW YOU'RE A COMPUTER NERD WHEN . . .

You double click your TV remote.

YOU KNOW YOU'RE A COMPUTER NERD WHEN . . .

You check your mail.
It says, 'No new
messages', so you
check it again,
and again.

YOU KNOW YOU'RE A COMPUTER NERD WHEN . . .

Your phone bill comes to your doorstep in a box.

YOU KNOW YOU'RE A COMPUTER NERD WHEN . . .

You can now type over 70 wpm.

YOU KNOW YOU'RE A COMPUTER NERD WHEN . . .

You don't know what gender three of your closest friends are, because they have neutral nicknames and you've never bothered to ask.

YOU KNOW YOU'RE A COMPUTER NERD WHEN . . .

You would rather tell people that your bloodshot eyes are from partying too much than the truth: you were on-line all night.

Net Addict

YOU KNOW YOU'RE A COMPUTER NERD WHEN . . .

You move into a new house and decide to Netscape before you landscape.

YOU KNOW YOU'RE A COMPUTER NERD WHEN . . .

You type messages to people while at the same time speaking to them on the phone.

YOU KNOW YOU'RE A COMPUTER NERD WHEN . . .

You find yourself lying to others about your time on-line and when they complain that your phone was busy you claim it was off the hook.

YOU KNOW YOU'RE A COMPUTER NERD WHEN . . .

Your dog has his own web page.

YOU KNOW YOU'RE A COMPUTER NERD WHEN . . .

Rex has got his own web page.

YOU KNOW YOU'RE A COMPUTER NERD WHEN . . .

So does your goldfish.

YOU KNOW YOU'RE A
COMPUTER NERD WHEN . . .

Your dog leaves you.

YOU KNOW YOU'RE A
COMPUTER NERD WHEN . . .

People keep telling you
to 'get a life'.

YOU KNOW YOU'RE A
COMPUTER NERD WHEN . . .

All your friends and
relatives give you blank
diskettes for your
birthday and Christmas
presents.

YOU KNOW YOU'RE A COMPUTER NERD WHEN . . .

You get in a lift and double-click the button for the floor you want.

YOU KNOW YOU'RE A COMPUTER NERD WHEN . . .

You start looking at new hard drives when you find you have less than 500 megs of space free on your present drive.

YOU KNOW YOU'RE A COMPUTER NERD WHEN . . .

You call your computer by a name.

YOU KNOW YOU'RE A COMPUTER NERD WHEN . . .

You wash your clothes
and find stray diskettes
in your pockets.

YOU KNOW YOU'RE A COMPUTER NERD WHEN . . .

You drop everything you're doing to go out and purchase the new program you just read about in a computer magazine.

YOU KNOW YOU'RE A COMPUTER NERD WHEN . . .

You hear the word 'windows' on the TV and turn up the volume only to find out it's an advert selling double glazing.

YOU KNOW YOU'RE A COMPUTER NERD WHEN . . .

You've become the person that everyone at work comes to with his or her computer problems.

YOU KNOW YOU'RE A COMPUTER NERD WHEN . . .

You look for an icon to
double click
to open your
bedroom window.

YOU KNOW YOU'RE A COMPUTER NERD WHEN . . .

You are actually proud of the fact that you are an addict.

YOU KNOW YOU'RE A COMPUTER NERD WHEN . . .

At dinner parties you always tell your friends that TWAIN stands for 'Tool Without An Interesting Name'.

You subscribe to more
than three monthly
computer magazines.

YOU KNOW YOU'RE A COMPUTER NERD WHEN . . .

You go out and buy 100 new floppies rather than go through the 300 used ones you have and delete the files on them.

YOU KNOW YOU'RE A COMPUTER NERD WHEN . . .

You own more than five books on the Internet.

YOU KNOW YOU'RE A
COMPUTER NERD WHEN . . .

You can't carry on a
conversation without
changing the subject
to computers.

YOU KNOW YOU'RE A COMPUTER NERD WHEN . . .

You are reading a book and look for the scroll bar to get to the next page.

YOU KNOW YOU'RE A COMPUTER NERD WHEN . . .

You start figuring 'must have' computer upgrades into the family budget.

YOU KNOW YOU'RE A COMPUTER NERD WHEN . . .

You have more computers in your home than there are people who live there.

YOU KNOW YOU'RE A COMPUTER NERD WHEN . . .

You upgrade your computer software packages as soon as a new one is available, even if you won't ever use the latest features.

YOU KNOW YOU'RE A COMPUTER NERD WHEN . . .

You begin to wonder how on earth your service provider is allowed to call 250 hours per month 'unlimited'.

YOU KNOW YOU'RE A COMPUTER NERD WHEN . . .

You have to get a second phone line just so you can call out for a pizza and stay on-line at the same time.

YOU KNOW YOU'RE A COMPUTER NERD WHEN . . .

You go up to people you are attracted to 'in real life' and ask them for their GIF.

YOU KNOW YOU'RE A
COMPUTER NERD WHEN . . .

You become insanely
jealous of people hitting
on your cyber-love.

You don't even know
what your cyber-love
looks like.

YOU KNOW YOU'RE A COMPUTER NERD WHEN . . .

Your children are eating cereal morning, noon and night.

YOU KNOW YOU'RE A COMPUTER NERD WHEN . . .

Instead of moaning about your snoring, your spouse now complains that you tap an imaginary keyboard in your sleep.

YOU KNOW YOU'RE A COMPUTER NERD WHEN . . .

When someone says, 'What did you say?' you reply, 'Scroll up!'

YOU KNOW YOU'RE A COMPUTER NERD WHEN . . .

You turn down the lights and close the curtains so people won't know you're on-line again.

YOU KNOW YOU'RE A COMPUTER NERD WHEN . . .

You send Internet Christmas cards to all your friends.

YOU KNOW YOU'RE A COMPUTER NERD WHEN . . .

You have an identity crisis if someone is using a screen name similar to your own.

YOU KNOW YOU'RE A COMPUTER NERD WHEN . . .

You change your screen names so much that you have to look at your own profile to see who you are.

You go into labour and you
stop to type a special
e-mail to let everyone
know you're going to be
away and how you're feeling.

YOU KNOW YOU'RE A
COMPUTER NERD WHEN . . .

You log on and
immediately get
ten IM's from people who
have you on their
'buddy list'.

YOU KNOW YOU'RE A COMPUTER NERD WHEN . . .

You talk to an annoying person in 'real life' and wish you had your 'ignore button' handy.

YOU KNOW YOU'RE A COMPUTER NERD WHEN . . .

You go into withdrawal if you are away from the computer for more than a few hours.

YOU KNOW YOU'RE A COMPUTER NERD WHEN . . .

You bring a packed lunch to the computer.

YOU KNOW YOU'RE A COMPUTER NERD WHEN . . .

Your best friend
is someone
you've never met.

YOU KNOW YOU'RE A COMPUTER NERD WHEN . . .

You never have to deal with busy signals when calling your ISP . . .

YOU KNOW YOU'RE A COMPUTER NERD WHEN . . .

Your on-line relationship has gone further than any real one you have ever had.

YOU KNOW YOU'RE A COMPUTER NERD WHEN . . .

You don't even notice any more when something has a typo.

YOU KNOW YOU'RE A COMPUTER NERD WHEN . . .

Someone tells you a joke and you silently write LOL on a piece of paper and hand it to them.

YOU KNOW YOU'RE A
COMPUTER NERD WHEN . . .

You start using phrases
like: Hungry.must-
eat.food.now@home

YOU KNOW YOU'RE A
COMPUTER NERD WHEN . . .

You enter a room and you
greet people with {{hugs}}
and **kisses**.

YOU KNOW YOU'RE A COMPUTER NERD WHEN . . .

You stop typing whole words and use things like 'ppl', 'dunno' and 'lemme'.

YOU KNOW YOU'RE A COMPUTER NERD WHEN . . .

Your voicemail/answering machine message is, 'BRB, leave your s/n and I will TTYL.'

YOU KNOW YOU'RE A COMPUTER NERD WHEN . . .

You dream in 'text'.

YOU KNOW YOU'RE A COMPUTER NERD WHEN . . .

You are on the phone and need to do something else so you say, 'BRB' or 'BBL'.

YOU KNOW YOU'RE A
COMPUTER NERD WHEN . . .

You go into withdrawal
during dinner.

YOU KNOW YOU'RE A
COMPUTER NERD WHEN . . .

You pay for software
to be delivered 'next
day' when you really
don't need it that quickly.

YOU KNOW YOU'RE A COMPUTER NERD WHEN . . .

You buy all the 'dummies' books for your wife/ husband to get them involved in computers.

YOU KNOW YOU'RE A COMPUTER NERD WHEN . . .

You name your computer as the co-respondent in your divorce papers.

YOU KNOW YOU'RE A COMPUTER NERD WHEN . . .

You stay on the Internet so much that your service provider makes you buy a corporate account.

YOU KNOW YOU'RE A COMPUTER NERD WHEN . . .

You get copies of programs from your friends and never use them.

YOU KNOW YOU'RE A
COMPUTER NERD WHEN . . .

You still refuse to delete
programs off your hard
drive that you haven't
used in two years.

YOU KNOW YOU'RE A
COMPUTER NERD WHEN . . .

You dream in pallettes of
256 colours.

YOU KNOW YOU'RE A COMPUTER NERD WHEN . . .

You take your computer on holiday with you, even if you go camping.

YOU KNOW YOU'RE A COMPUTER NERD WHEN . . .

You memorise the telephone numbers of your favourite computer stores.

YOU KNOW YOU'RE A COMPUTER NERD WHEN . . .

You try to sleep, and think: sleep(8*3600)/ *sleep for 8 hours/

YOU KNOW YOU'RE A COMPUTER NERD WHEN . . .

You ask your doctor to implant a gig in your brain.

YOU KNOW YOU'RE A COMPUTER NERD WHEN . . .

You can type your top ten favourite websites, by heart.

YOU KNOW YOU'RE A COMPUTER NERD WHEN . . .

All your daydreaming is preoccupied with getting a faster connection to the Net.

YOU KNOW YOU'RE A
COMPUTER NERD WHEN . . .

You type faster
than you think.

YOU KNOW YOU'RE A COMPUTER NERD WHEN . . .

You can actually read and follow all the names of the cast that scroll up your TV screen at the end of a film.

YOU KNOW YOU'RE A COMPUTER NERD WHEN . . .

Your Net provider suggests you try a competitor, because you're exceeding 300 hours a month, connect time.

YOU KNOW YOU'RE A COMPUTER NERD WHEN . . .

You have more than
five e-mail addresses.

YOU KNOW YOU'RE A COMPUTER NERD WHEN . . .

Your 112Gb hard drive is full.

YOU KNOW YOU'RE A COMPUTER NERD WHEN . . .

You modify the programming of your car's computers and actually get better mileage.

YOU KNOW YOU'RE A COMPUTER NERD WHEN . . .

Your fingers seize up because you've been on-line for 36 hours.

YOU KNOW YOU'RE A COMPUTER NERD WHEN . . .

You log off from a session in your favourite newsgroup and your log reads: On-line time: 56 hours 24 minutes.

YOU KNOW YOU'RE A COMPUTER NERD WHEN . . .

Your bookmark takes 10 minutes to scroll from top to bottom.

YOU KNOW YOU'RE A COMPUTER NERD WHEN . . .

You kiss your loved one's home page.

YOU KNOW YOU'RE A COMPUTER NERD WHEN . . .

Net Addict

You code your homework in HTML and give your teacher the URL.

YOU KNOW YOU'RE A
COMPUTER NERD WHEN . . .

You find yourself
brainstorming for new
subjects to search.

YOU KNOW YOU'RE A COMPUTER NERD WHEN . . .

You've already visited all the links at Yahoo and you're halfway through Lycos.

YOU KNOW YOU'RE A COMPUTER NERD WHEN . . .

Smoke starts billowing out of your modem.

**For the latest humour books
from Summersdale, check out**

www.summersdale.com